MAKO SHARK

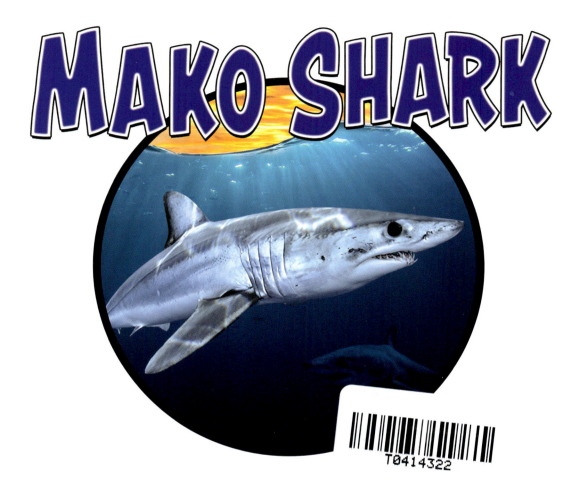

By Jennifer Boothroyd

Consultant: Erin McCombs
Educator, Aquarium of the Pacific

Minneapolis, Minnesota

Credits

Cover and title page, © wildestanimal/Shutterstock, © Rich Carey/Shutterstock, © I AM NIKOM/Shutterstock; 3, © nabil refaat/Shutterstock; 4-5, © Martin Prochazkacz/Shutterstock; 5, © Rich Carey/Shutterstock; 6-7, © divedog/Shutterstock; 8-9, © Nature Picture Library /Alamy; 10-11, © Richard Robinson/Getty; 12-13, © Ronald C. Modra/Getty; 14-15, © Ryan Cake/Getty; 15, © apomares/iStockPhoto; 16-17, © Nature Picture Library / Alamy; 18-19, © Image Source/Alamy; 20-21, © WaterFrame/Alamy; 22, © wildestanimal/Shutterstock; 22-23, © nabil refaat/Shutterstock; 24, © nabil refaat/Shutterstock.

President: Jen Jenson
Director of Product Development: Spencer Brinker
Senior Editor: Allison Juda
Associate Editor: Charly Haley
Designer: Colin O'Dea

Library of Congress Cataloging-in-Publication Data

Names: Boothroyd, Jennifer, 1972- author.
Title: Mako shark / by Jennifer Boothroyd.
Description: Minneapolis, Minnesota : Bearport Publishing Company, [2022] | Series: Shark shock! | Includes bibliographical references and index.
Identifiers: LCCN 2021039175 (print) | LCCN 2021039176 (ebook) | ISBN 9781636915333 (library binding) | ISBN 9781636915425 (paperback) | ISBN 9781636915517 (ebook)
Subjects: LCSH: Mako sharks--Juvenile literature.
Classification: LCC QL638.95.L3 B66 2022 (print) | LCC QL638.95.L3 (ebook) | DDC 597.3--dc23
LC record available at https://lccn.loc.gov/2021039175
LC ebook record available at https://lccn.loc.gov/2021039176

Copyright © 2022 Bearport Publishing Company. All rights reserved. No part of this publication may be reproduced in whole or in part, stored in any retrieval system, or transmitted in any form or by any means, electronic, mechanical, photocopying, recording, or otherwise, without written permission from the publisher.

For more information, write to Bearport Publishing, 5357 Penn Avenue South, Minneapolis, MN 55419. Printed in the United States of America.

Contents

Look Out Below! 4
Two Makos 6
Long and Narrow 8
Warm and Fast 10
A Shark Out of Water 12
On the Hunt 14
What's on the Menu? 16
Makos in Danger 18
The Life of a Mako Shark 20

More about Mako Sharks 22
Glossary 23
Index 24
Read More 24
Learn More Online 24
About the Author 24

Look Out Below!

A group of tuna swims through the ocean. The fish cannot see a mako shark lurking beneath them. This sneaky hunter quietly follows the fish. Then, the mako begins swimming in circles below its **prey**. Suddenly—with a burst of speed—the shark rushes up and bites into a tuna. *Chomp!*

> Mako sharks can see very well in dark waters, which helps them hide as they follow their prey.

Tuna

Two Makos

Mako sharks live in oceans all over the world. There are two kinds of mako sharks. Shortfin makos are easier to spot. They can be found near the **coast** in some places. Longfin makos are more **rare**. They live in deeper parts of the oceans. But both kinds of mako sharks swim long distances across the oceans, often swimming many miles a day.

Longfin makos have longer front fins and larger eyes than shortfin makos do.

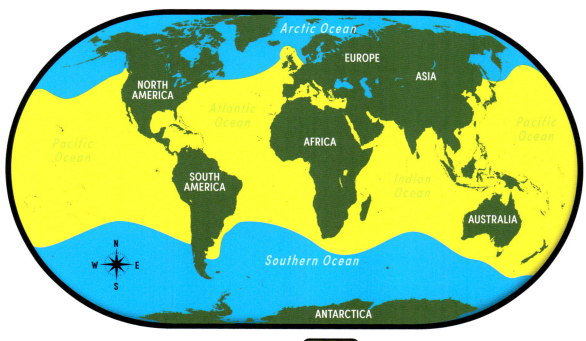

Long and Narrow

Mako sharks easily cut through the waters with their long, narrow bodies. Shortfin makos can be up to 13 ft (4 m) long. Longfins are often bigger—they can get up to 14 ft (4.3 m) long. And mako sharks are heavy, too. They can weigh more than a grand piano.

One of the heaviest shortfin makos ever found weighed 1,300 pounds (600 kg).

Warm and Fast

Unlike most sharks, makos are partly **warm-blooded**. They can heat some of their blood to warm their **muscles**. This lets makos swim faster and farther than other sharks. In fact, mako sharks are among the fastest fish in the world! They usually swim at about 22 miles per hour (35 kph).

At their fastest, shortfin mako sharks can swim more than 45 miles per hour (70 kph)!

A Shark Out of Water

Shortfin makos use their speed to jump out of water! Sometimes, they do this when catching prey from below. The sharks quickly swim up toward prey near the water's **surface**. Then, strong muscles and a special tail fin help them jump above the waves. Makos can jump 20 to 30 ft (6 to 9 m) in the air.

Some mako sharks have even jumped into fishing boats.

On the Hunt

Jumping is not the only thing that makes these sharks great hunters. Their coloring helps them hide as they swim below prey. From above, a mako's dark blue back blends in with the dark water. Then, when this hunter is ready to catch its meal, it swims up and sinks its teeth into the prey's tail or belly.

Makos have long, pointy teeth. Many of their bottom teeth stick out, even when their mouths are closed!

What's on the Menu?

Makos eat mostly bluefish, tuna, and swordfish. These are some of the fastest fish in the ocean, so the sharks' speed is important for hunting. They chase groups of fish for miles.

Do any animals eat makos? No! Luckily for them, these sharks are at the top of the **food chain**.

Sometimes mako sharks' prey will fight back! Some makos even have scars from being stabbed by the sharp points of swordfish.

Makos in Danger

Mako sharks may not be hunted by creatures in the ocean, but they are still in danger because of humans. Many people fish for shortfin mako sharks.

Mako sharks are often caught accidentally, too. They end up in large fishing nets used to catch tuna and swordfish. Because of fishing, the number of mako sharks in the world is getting smaller.

People hunt makos, but these sharks do not hunt humans.

The Life of a Mako Shark

Mako sharks are in the most danger when they are at their smallest. Baby shortfin makos grow inside their mothers for about a year and a half before they are born. But the newborn **pups** are still only a few feet long. They grow bigger as they eat and get older.

Mako sharks can live for about 30 years.

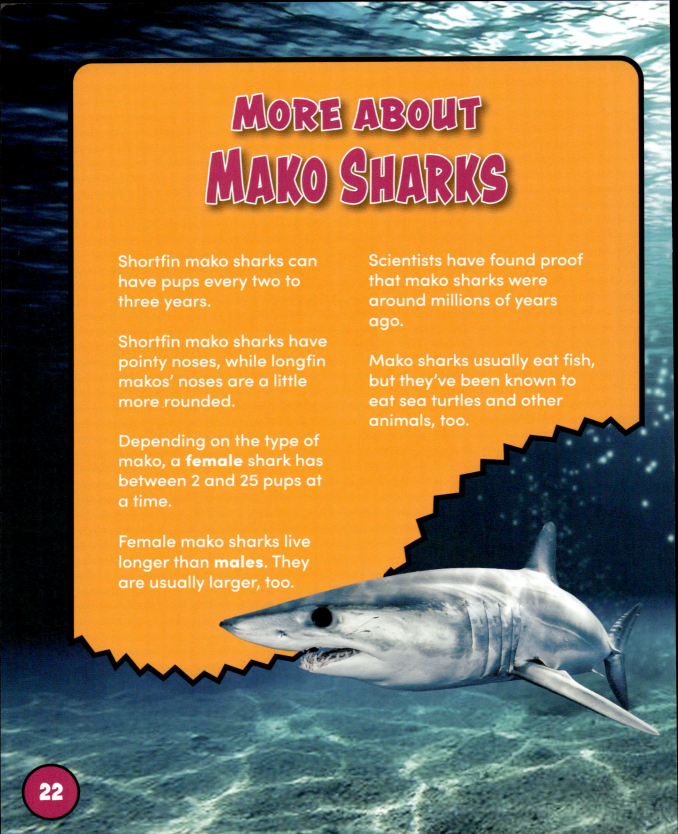

More About Mako Sharks

Shortfin mako sharks can have pups every two to three years.

Shortfin mako sharks have pointy noses, while longfin makos' noses are a little more rounded.

Depending on the type of mako, a **female** shark has between 2 and 25 pups at a time.

Female mako sharks live longer than **males**. They are usually larger, too.

Scientists have found proof that mako sharks were around millions of years ago.

Mako sharks usually eat fish, but they've been known to eat sea turtles and other animals, too.

Glossary

coast an area where land meets an ocean

female a mako shark that can give birth to young

food chain a series of plants and animals that depend on one another for food

males mako sharks that cannot give birth to young

muscles parts of the body that make it move

prey animals that are hunted and eaten by other animals

pups baby sharks

rare not common

surface the top of water

warm-blooded having blood that can stay the same temperature no matter the temperature of the environment

Index

eyes 6
fins 6, 12
hunting 4, 14, 16, 18–19
jumping 12–14
muscles 10, 12
oceans 4, 6–7, 16, 18
people 18–19
prey 4, 12, 14, 17
pups 20, 22
swordfish 16–18
teeth 14–15
tuna 4–5, 16, 18

Read More

Nixon, Madeline. *Mako Shark (Sharks)*. New York: AV2, 2019.

Pettiford, Rebecca. *Mako Sharks (Blastoff! Readers: Shark Frenzy)*. Minneapolis: Bellwether Media, 2021.

Learn More Online

1. Go to **www.factsurfer.com** or scan the QR code below.
2. Enter **"Mako Shark"** into the search box.
3. Click on the cover of this book to see a list of websites.

About the Author

Jennifer Boothroyd has helped kids learn about nature for more than 25 years. While she has swum in oceans many times, she has never seen a shark in the wild.